OUR PLANET

Weather

DAVID LAMBERT

Troll Associates

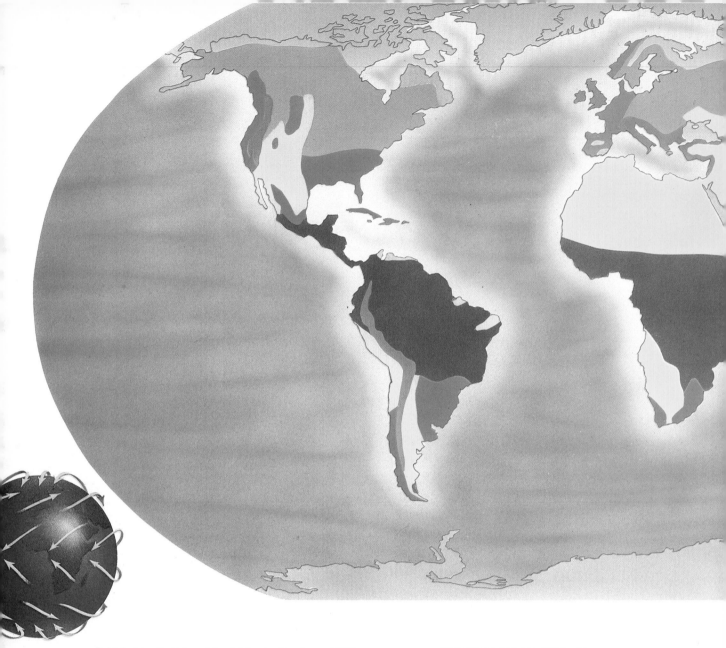

Published by Troll Associates, Mahwah, New Jersey 07430

Design by James Marks, London.

Picture research by Jan Croot.

Illustrators: Mike Roffe: pages 4-5, 8, 10-11, 12, 14-15, 17, 18, 24-25, 26; Paul Sullivan: pages 22-23; Ian Thompson: pages 2-3.

Printed in the U.S.A.

10 9 8 7 6 5 4 3 2 1

Library of Congress Cataloging-in-Publication Data

Lambert, David, (date)
    Weather / by David Lambert; illustrated by Martin Camm . . . [et al.].
        p.   cm.—(Our planet)
    Summary: Describes factors that influence our climate and weather.
    ISBN 0-8167-1979-9 (lib. bdg.)   ISBN 0-8167-1980-2 (pbk.)
    1. Weather—Juvenile literature.   [1. Weather.   2. Climatology.]
I. Camm, Martin, ill. II. Title. III. Series.
QC981.3.L35 1990
551.6—dc20   89-20304

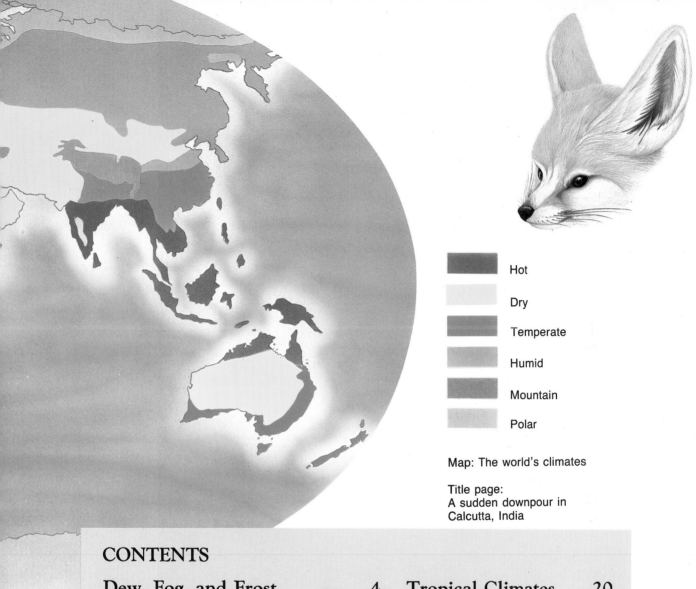

Hot

Dry

Temperate

Humid

Mountain

Polar

Map: The world's climates

Title page:
A sudden downpour in
Calcutta, India

CONTENTS

Dew, Fog and Frost

Have you ever forgotten a saucepan of water on the stove and returned to find the saucepan empty? Where did the water go? It *evaporated*, or changed into *water vapor*, an invisible gas which was absorbed by the air in your kitchen.

Much the same happens in nature. The sun's heat makes water from seas, lakes, and rivers evaporate and rise into the *atmosphere*, the blanket of air surrounding the Earth.

↑ Frost and ice on trees after a freezing winter night. Weather scientists measure ground frost at grass level, and air frost at a height of 4½ feet.

When air has absorbed all the water it can hold, it is said to be *saturated*. The warmer the air is, the more moisture it can hold. As saturated air cools, some of the water vapor in it *condenses*, or changes into tiny droplets of water. The temperature at which condensation happens is called the *dew point*.

If it turns chilly at night, water vapor in the air condenses as the air touches the cold ground. Next morning we find the ground covered with dew, or with frost if the temperature is freezing.

Fog is a dense cloud of water droplets hanging just above the ground; a thinner cloud is mist.

→ Snowblower clearing an airport runway. Snow, frost and fog often cause problems for travelers.

Rain, Snow, Sleet, and Hail

High in the sky, water vapor from seas, lakes, and rivers condenses on particles drifting in the air. These include specks of dust, smoke from chimneys, and salt from the sea. Because it's cold in the sky, moisture in the atmosphere can also turn into ice.

Clouds are millions of tiny, lightweight water droplets or ice crystals floating together. In warm clouds, droplets bumping into each other make larger and larger drops of water. These are too heavy to stay up, so they fall from the cloud as rain.

Snowflakes are formed in colder clouds, by ice crystals sticking together. The flakes are always six-sided, though no two look exactly alike. If there is warm air below, snowflakes and ice crystals falling from clouds melt on the way down and turn into sleet or rain.

When ice crystals are hurled up and down in a storm cloud, they grow into hailstones. Freezing water droplets stick to the crystals, adding layers of clear and frosty ice. You don't often see hailstones bigger than cherries, but the "stones" can be as large as tennis balls and can weigh over 2 pounds.

← Different kinds of clouds are found at different heights in the sky. From 3 to 8 miles up: wispy, white, *high-level clouds,* made of ice crystals. From 1 to 4 miles: thicker, white, *medium-level* clouds, containing ice and water. Less than 1 mile up: dull, gray, *low-level clouds,* made of water droplets only. Shapely *cumulus* clouds and towering *cumulonimbus* storm clouds form lower down, but often drift upward.

Rain, snow, and hail are all part of the *water cycle,* the two-way flow of water between the Earth's surface and the atmosphere. Water vapor from seas, lakes, and rivers rises into the sky, then returns to Earth as rain, snow, or hail. Rainwater and melted snow or hail fill up the seas, lakes, and rivers – and so the cycle continues, without ever ending.

Winds

Wind is moving air, and air movements are caused by differences in *air pressure* and temperature. Air pressure is the weight of air pressing down on the Earth's surface. Winds flow from high-pressure to low-pressure areas. Pressure is high where air sinks and low where it rises.

Temperature differences make air move because warm air is light and cold air is heavy. So cold air always flows in to replace warm air that is rising. One place where this happens is the seashore during hot weather. Land warms up faster than water, so a sea breeze blows towards the shore in the morning. At night a land breeze blows out to sea, because the water takes longer to cool.

↑ The flow of air between the equator and the poles gives the world's main winds a regular pattern. The twisting shape is due to the Earth's spin.

Winds range from gentle breezes to great rivers of air that blow around the world. From the equator, warm air rises and spreads out over the tropics. From the edges of the tropics, strong, steady *trade winds* blow back toward the equator and mild westerly winds blow toward the North and South Poles.

When cold *easterlies* from the poles clash with warm *westerlies*, the winds whirl around each other as *cyclones* (also known as *depressions*). These spirals of

→ Cyclones bring unsettled or stormy weather. These spirals of wind and clouds are often hundreds of miles wide.

↑ Balloons are carried great distances by the wind. Hot air balloons rise because air becomes lighter when heated.

low-pressure air bring cloudy or windy weather and rain or snow. At the edge of the tropics, air from the equator cools and sinks, creating spirals of high-pressure air called *anticyclones*. Anticyclones bring clear skies and sunshine in summer. In winter, they can bring bright cold weather, frost, and fog.

Wild Weather

Thunderstorms unleash enormous power and energy. Lightning is a massive electric spark jumping between clouds or from a cloud to the ground. Thunder and lightning happen at the same moment, but the lightning seems to come first because light travels faster than sound. Lightning heats air to as much as 86,000°F. The intense heat makes the air expand with a bang or a rumble.

Hurricanes are violent storms produced by moist air and heat rising from tropical seas in late summer. As the hot air escapes upward, cool air spirals in to replace it because of the Earth's spin. Moisture in the rising air condenses into clouds, and after several hours or days the storm begins. At the center of the spiral is a calm spot called the *eye*. Around it, winds whirl at up to 200 miles per hour.

Tornadoes are like mini-hurricanes, but they start over land. Because they are so concentrated, tornadoes are even more violent than hurricanes.

← A tornado is a spinning funnel of air hanging from a thundercloud. Small tornadoes may be only 150 feet wide at the ground, but the largest are more than 1,500 feet wide. Their winds can reach over 400 miles per hour – strong enough to pick up cars and make buildings explode.

→ Lightning flashing between a cloud and the city below.

Forecasting the Weather

Once, people could only guess what tomorrow's weather would be like. Now, scientists can forecast the weather fairly accurately, though they do not always get it right. In 1987, only hours before England was struck by a hurricane, a forecaster reassured television viewers that a hurricane was not expected!

Forecasts help farmers plan work on their crops. Pilots can be told how to make the best use of the winds. We can plan outings and holidays, and people can stock up on food if a bad storm is forecast.

Correct forecasting needs weather information, night and day, from places all around the world. This is collected from manned and unmanned weather stations on land and at sea. *Meteorologists*, or weather scientists, use a variety of instruments to record air temperature and pressure, humidity (moisture in the air), and wind speed. Instruments sent up by balloon give radio reports of weather in the upper air. Radar screens show approaching showers and storms.

Satellites now gaze down upon the world's weather, like ever-open eyes in the sky. Their instruments monitor all weather changes. They can spot waves ruffled by the wind or the beginnings of a hurricane.

→ By making observations, you can measure the weather in your area and even make your own forecasts. To set up a weather station, you will need special instruments. A *thermometer* measures temperature. A *rain gauge* measures depth of rain; a marked-off flat-bottomed jar will do this. An *arrow vane* shows wind direction. An *anemometer* measures wind speed; wind blows the cups around, and you can count the number of turns per minute. You can record the weather on a wall chart or in a diary. In dry weather, seaweed curls and pine cones open up. If you collect some, you can see how the weather affects them.

↑ Pictures of clouds taken by weather satellites are shown on TV weather forecasts. This satellite is over North America and the Gulf of Mexico.

Satellites beam all this information in code back to Earth. Receiving equipment on the ground turns the information into weather maps displayed on screens. To forecast the world's weather for the next 24 hours means making about 500 million calculations. Only the world's most powerful supercomputers work fast enough to tackle such a gigantic task.

Making a Forecast

Even forecasting one country's weather involves gathering thousands of measurements from land, air, sea, and space. Meteorologists use these measurements to build a complete picture of the present weather. They pay special attention to changes in pressure, as these provide information about the huge air movements which control our weather. From present conditions, forecasters work out likely weather changes in different parts of the country after "time steps" of 10 minutes, 20 minutes, and so on.

Supercomputers provide details of the weather as numbers. Meteorologists use these numbers to make weather charts. These are maps with lines, arrows, and other symbols showing air pressure, temperatures, winds, clouds, sun, fog, and rain, sleet, or snow.

Weather can be forecast correctly by computers several days ahead. Beyond that, even small errors in the information they are given may result in forecasts being totally wrong.

→ Hurricane damage in Texas. Forecasts can give warning of storms.

↓ Weather centers collect information from radar, balloons, satellites, aircraft, ships and unmanned weather stations.

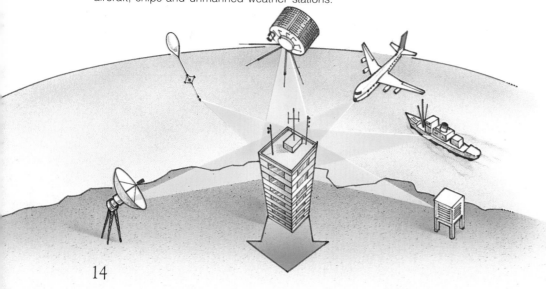

14

Putting Weather to Work

Sunshine brings us more energy in a week than lies locked up in all the Earth's oil, gas, coal, and uranium. Engineers can use this *solar energy* (energy from the sun) to heat and light homes, offices, and factories.

In the sunnier countries, solar panels on the roofs of houses are often used for heating water. Similarly, big solar power plants use mirrors to reflect the sun's rays onto water tanks and pipes. As the water boils, it produces steam that spins turbine blades to generate electric current. Years from now, sunshine reflected by huge mirrors in space may light whole cities at night.

On windy hills and coasts, engineers sometimes build windmills called *aerogenerators* that use the power of the

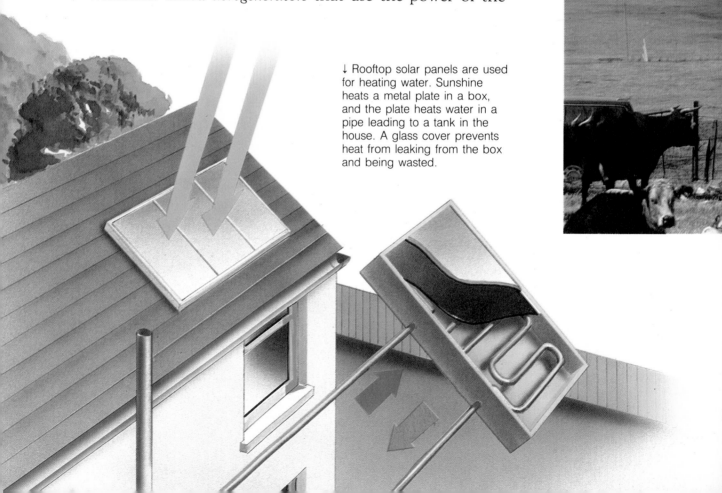

↓ Rooftop solar panels are used for heating water. Sunshine heats a metal plate in a box, and the plate heats water in a pipe leading to a tank in the house. A glass cover prevents heat from leaking from the box and being wasted.

↑ Rows of *aerogenerators* on a *wind farm* in California. When the wind stops blowing, these small windmills switch over to their batteries, where the current is stored, to keep the supply going. Wind power is cheap and does not cause pollution. A large wind farm can provide electricity for a whole town.

wind to make electricity. As yet, solar energy and wind power meet only a small part of our needs. But they are bound to become more common as we use up fuels such as coal, oil, and natural gas that we cannot replace. Many people believe nuclear power is too dangerous, so the search for a new and safer energy source continues.

Changing the Weather

People not only put weather to work, they also change it — sometimes for better, sometimes for worse.

In sunny cities such as Los Angeles, fumes from truck and car exhausts produce dirty brownish fog, or "smog." In industrial cities, smoke and gas from factory chimneys can cause choking yellow smog, like the kind that killed 2,850 Londoners in 1952. These fumes and gases make rain turn as acid as vinegar. In Canada and many parts of Europe, acid rain has killed whole forests and thousands of freshwater fish.

To protect their crops, farmers tamper with the weather. On cold spring nights, fruit growers spray orange groves with a mist of water droplets. The misty air traps heat, so the orange blossom isn't killed by frost. After weeks without rain, *cloud seeding* can save drought-stricken crops and cattle. Planes "seed" clouds by spraying them with crystals, in the hope that moisture will stick to the crystals and fall as rain. However, rainmaking does not always work.

Our actions do not only affect day-to-day weather. They can even alter *climate*, the general weather pattern of a region over a long period of time.

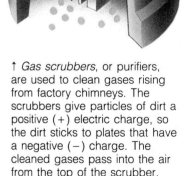

↑ *Gas scrubbers*, or purifiers, are used to clean gases rising from factory chimneys. The scrubbers give particles of dirt a positive (+) electric charge, so the dirt sticks to plates that have a negative (−) charge. The cleaned gases pass into the air from the top of the scrubber.

← The Golden Gate Bridge, San Francisco, surrounded by fog. The California coast is foggy because the ocean cools warm air rising from the coastal cities.

Tropical Climates

Parts of the tropics near the equator have a hot, damp climate. Because the temperature changes very little, the seasons hardly vary. Cocoa, rubber, and tropical fruits, such as bananas and coconuts, thrive there. So do rain forests rich in wildlife, such as monkeys, snakes, and colorful birds and butterflies.

But not all places in the tropics are like this. Mountainous regions, where coffee and tea are grown, have cooler climates. Also, not far from the equator, there are *monsoon lands*, which have a two-season year. During part of the year, when the winds blow out to sea, the weather is warm and dry. Then the winds reverse direction, and for weeks or months there is heavy rain. Monsoon lands are found in Asia, Africa, and South America. Many of them have *savannas*, or vast, flat grasslands. In places, the grass can be twice as tall as a man. The African savannas have a great variety of wildlife, including lions, giraffes, and elephants. Large herds of zebras and antelopes roam these wide, open plains.

Beyond the monsoon lands, vegetation becomes sparser, and at the edges of the tropics there are hot, dry deserts.

→ The gibbon is a small ape found in the tropical rain forests of Southeast Asia. Gibbons feed on fruit and leaves, and use their long arms to swing from branch to branch. They live in family groups.

20

↑ Harvesting on the tropical island of Bali, in Indonesia. In the tropics the sun shines down strongly from high in the sky, so farm workers often wear large straw hats to shield their heads from its heat.

→ The arrow-poison frog lives in the tropical rain forests of Central and South America. Amerindians dip the tips of their arrows in the deadly poison produced by its skin. The frog's brilliant colors warn other animals that it is poisonous.

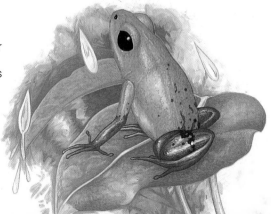

↑ A young camel feeding on its mother's milk near the edge of the Arabian Desert. Camels are well-adapted to living in hot, dry deserts. They can drink up to 13 gallons of water at a time.

People used to believe that camels stored water in their humps. In fact, they use the humps to store fat, which allows them to survive for days without eating.

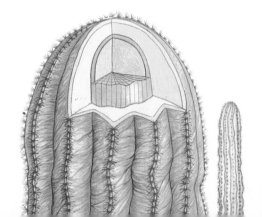

22

Hot Deserts

Hot deserts cover almost a third of the world's land, stretching across parts of Africa, Arabia, North and South America, India, and Australia. In the daytime it is so hot that you can fry eggs on the rocks. But winter nights can be frosty, for after dark the heat quickly vanishes into the cloudless sky.

To scientists, a desert is an area where the average rainfall is less than 10 inches a year. *Droughts*, periods without rain, can last for months or years. Parts of Chile's Atacama Desert actually stayed dry for 400 years until rain fell in 1971.

Desert plants and animals have ways of coping with the hot, dry climate. Cacti store water in fat, juicy stems. Mice and lizards lick dew from pebbles. Many animals burrow during the day to escape from the sun.

When forests are destroyed or land is misused, the soil dries out and can turn into desert. The Sahara, the world's biggest desert, is steadily spreading southward; in Australia, 10 million acres of farmland are rapidly turning into dust. If deserts continue to spread at the present rate, by the end of this century they will have swallowed up a third of the land where crops once grew.

↑ The fennec lives in the Sahara and Arabian Deserts. Its large ears have a network of veins close to the skin so the wind keeps its blood cool.

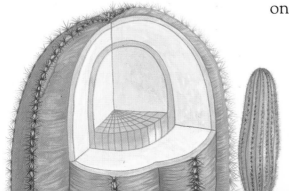

← Like many other desert plants, cacti soak up amazing amounts of water from rare showers. They store the water in their spongy stems. Their skin is ribbed so it can expand **(right)**, as the cactus takes in water.

23

Temperate Climates

Cold air from the poles and warm air from the tropics fight above much of North America and Europe, and over southern parts of Australia and South America. This weather war produces climates that are *temperate* – neither burning hot nor freezing cold.

The British Isles, many European countries, New Zealand, and much of western North America have cool temperate climates. Both deciduous trees (trees that shed all their leaves every year) and evergreens grow there. The cool climate is suitable for many kinds of crops and is particularly good for dairy farming.

Since they are nearer to the tropics, southern California and the Mediterranean countries enjoy a warm temperate climate, with mild winters and warm summers. Grapes, peaches, and oranges are grown in California and around the Mediterranean, as there is plenty of sun to ripen the fruit.

Living closer to the North Pole, people in Scandinavia and the north of Canada have to put up with short

Evergreen trees

Deciduous trees

↑ Rolled-up bales of hay on a farm in Wales. The trees and fields are typical of a cool temperate climate.

← Both deciduous trees and evergreens grow well in cool temperate climates.

summers and long, snowy winters. These northern lands have forests of fir trees and other conifers that can stand the cold. The central plains of North America and Russia have hotter summers. Much of the land there is used for growing wheat.

25

← The hooded seal swims in deep Arctic waters. When fully grown, it is about 10 feet long. Some seals live on and around the coasts of Antarctica.

↑ Polar bears live in the frozen Arctic, feeding on seals, fish, and birds. They can be up to 9 feet long and weigh 1,500 pounds.

Life at the Poles

Toes and fingers can freeze and drop off in the world's coldest climates. The Arctic and Antarctic, the regions around the North and South Poles, are the coldest places on Earth.

In winter, a blanket of ice smothers the entire Arctic Ocean. Ice sheets, in places almost 2½ miles thick, cover the continent of Antarctica all year.

Polar regions are so cold because they get little warmth from the sun. At the poles, the sun only peeps over the skyline for half the year. During the rest of the year, it is never seen. Even in summer, the sun's rays are too weak to melt much of the ice.

The wildlife of the Arctic includes polar bears and white-coated foxes. Various birds and mammals breed there in the summer, and hundreds of small plants burst into color when the snow thaws in the spring. In Antarctica, seals and penguins live on the coast; but apart from certain mosses and insects, hardly anything can survive inland. Oil workers, hunters, and fishermen live in the Arctic, but only scientists stay long on frozen Antarctica.

↑ The Emperor penguin lives and breeds on Antarctic coasts. The largest seabird on Earth, it is almost 4 feet tall when fully grown.

← The Arctic fox grows a coat of thick white fur in winter. It feeds on birds, lemmings, and Arctic hares.

27

Climates to Come

Once, ice smothered the land where New York stands, and Antarctica was warm enough for dinosaurs to live there. Just as the Earth's climates have changed, so they will undoubtedly alter again.

Today, the Earth is becoming warmer because we burn so much wood, oil, gas, and coal. These fuels give off carbon dioxide, which hangs in the air like an invisible blanket trapping the sun's heat. This is called the *greenhouse effect*. If the world warms up much more, parts of the polar ice sheets will melt. Then the seas will rise, swamping low-lying towns and countries. Since trees soak up carbon dioxide, the destruction of forests also adds to the greenhouse effect.

Another danger is from gases called CFCs, which are used in refrigerators and aerosol sprays. These gases rise into the sky and damage the layer of ozone around the Earth that shields us from harmful ultra-violet rays from the sun. Some governments are now acting to stop this threat to our health.

In a thousand years, a new ice age could grip northern lands. Scientists believe ice ages happen when, for a time, the Earth moves slightly further away from the sun, so less sunshine reaches the Earth.

Many millions of years from now, overheating will be the problem as the sun swells and blazes down on the Earth. When this happens, our planet will perish. Oceans will boil away, rocks will melt, and air will vanish into space.

→ Millions of years from now, when the heat of the sun increases, the surface of the Earth could look like this.

Fact File

Sunshine
Life on Earth depends on sunshine. We are 93 million miles from the sun. If we were nearer we would roast; if we were further away, all of the Earth would be frozen.

Most and Least Sunshine
The sunniest place on Earth is the eastern Sahara Desert in Africa, which averages nearly 12 hours of sunshine a day. The least sunny place is the North Pole, where the sun is not seen for half the year.

Hottest Places
The highest temperature ever recorded was 136.4°F in Libya in 1922. The second hottest temperature recorded was 134°F in Death Valley, California, in 1913.

From 1960 to 1966, at Dallol in Ethiopia the average annual temperature was 94°F.

Coldest Places
The lowest temperature ever recorded was −128°F at Vostok, the Russian scientific base in Antarctica, in 1983.

In January 1916, the temperature at Browning, Montana fell from 44°F to −56°F during a single day.

Wettest Places
The wettest place in the world is Tutunendo, Colombia, in South America, with an average rainfall of 463 inches per year. Mount Waialeale in Hawaii has had as many as 350 rainy days in a year.

Snowiest Places
From February 1971 to February 1972, Paradise on Mount Rainier in the state of Washington received 102 feet of snow. The deepest snow ever reported was 28 feet on Lassen Peak, California, in April 1983.

Strongest Winds
The world's windiest places are parts of Antarctica, where winds often reach 200 miles per hour.

The strongest winds are those of some tornadoes. These are difficult to measure accurately, as they damage most recording instruments, but it is estimated that they can reach more than 400 miles per hour.

Lightning
A flash of lightning can be 20 miles long and five times hotter than the sun, yet it may be only ½ inch wide at its core.

Light travels nearly 186,000 miles per second, but it takes sound about 5 seconds to travel 1 mile. This is why you see lightning before you hear thunder. If you count the seconds between lightning and thunder, then divide the number by five, that tells you how many miles away the storm is.

Longest Drought
Droughts are long periods without any rain. The longest drought, in Chile's Atacama Desert, lasted 400 years, until rain fell in 1971.

↓ *Dry soil during a drought*

Floods

Floods are usually caused by rivers rising after heavy rain or by the sea swamping the land. In 1887, nearly 1 million people drowned when the Yellow River in China overflowed its banks. In 1970, flooding after heavy rains drowned a similar number of people in Bangladesh.

Rainbows

Rainbows appear when there is sun and rain at the same time, and you are between the two with the sun at your back. The raindrops split the sun's rays into bands of red, orange, yellow, green, blue, indigo, and violet light. You can remember the colors if you think of their first letters as spelling ROYGBIV. Rainbows gradually fade as the rain stops falling.

Mirages

When light bends as it passes through layers of dense and less dense air, people sometimes see mirages – things that are not really there. For example, you may see a puddle of water that is really the sky reflected by hot air just above the surface of a road. Another common mirage is when distant mountains or oases appear in the middle of an empty desert.

Auroras

These are flickering bands of colored light that move across the sky. They are caused by conditions in the atmosphere high above the Earth, and are most commonly seen near the North and South Poles.

↑ *Aurora, seen from Alaska*

↓ *Rainbow*

Index

Picture Credits
Hutchison Library: Maurice Harvey pages 8-9;
Nigel Smith 16-17; Bernard Régent 18-19;
Jeremy Horner 20-21; Victor Lamont 30
Royal Geographical Society: 22-23
Science Photo Library:
Earth Satellite Corporation 13;
Jack Finch 31 (top)
Frank Spooner Pictures:
Christopher Harris 14-15
Survival Anglia: Dieter & Mary Plage 4;
T.D. Timms 24-25; Jack Lentfer 26-27
Zefa (UK) Ltd: 1, 4-5, 10-11, 31 (bottom)